Glorify Thy Name

Glorify Thy Name

A Forty-Day Study of Prayers in Scripture

Heather Jean
Wilson Torosyan

COMMUNITY CHRISTIAN MINISTRIES
MOSCOW, IDAHO

Community Christian Ministries
P.O. Box 9754, Moscow, Idaho 83843
208.883.0997 | www.ccmbooks.org

Heather Jean Wilson Torosyan, *Glorify Thy Name: A Forty-Day Study of
Prayers in Scripture*

ISBN: 978-1-882840-43-4

Cover design by Samuel Dickison.
Interior design by Valerie Anne Bost.
Printed in the United States of America.

22 23 24 25 26 27 28 29 30 31   10 9 8 7 6 5 4 3 2 1

Lord, glorify Your name in my life.

Contents

Foreword **ix**

Preface **xi**

SECTION ONE
The Teaching & Prayers of Jesus

Day 1 (*Matt. 6:6–8*)	**3**	Day 7 (*John 17:6–12*)	**25**
Day 2 (*Matt. 6:9–13*)	**5**	Day 8 (*Psalm 29:1–9*)	**29**
Day 3 (*Matt. 26:29*)	**9**	Day 9 (*John 17:13–21*)	**33**
Day 4 (*Luke 23:34*)	**13**	Day 10 (*John 17:22–26*)	**37**
Day 5 (*John 12:27–28*)	**17**	Day 11 (*Luke 18:10–14*)	**41**
Day 6 (*John 17:1–5*)	**21**	Day 12 (*Luke 10:21*)	**45**

SECTION TWO
The Prayers of Paul

Day 13 (*Rom. 1:8–10*)	**49**	Day 19 (*1 Thess. 5:23–25*)	**67**
Day 14 (*1 Cor. 1:4–9*)	**53**	Day 20 (*2 Thess. 1:3, 11–12*)	**69**
Day 15 (*2 Cor. 1:10–11*)	**57**	Day 21 (*1 Tim. 1:17*)	**71**
Day 16 (*Eph. 1:15–19*)	**59**	Day 22 (*1 Tim. 2:1–4*)	**73**
Day 17 (*Phil. 1:9–11*)	**61**	Day 23 (*2 Tim. 1:3*)	**75**
Day 18 (*Col. 1:9–12*)	**63**	Day 24 (*Heb. 13:20–21*)	**77**

SECTION THREE
The Prayers of the Old Testament

Day 25 *(Gen. 32:24–30)* **81**

Day 26 *(Exod. 33:12–15)* **85**

Day 27 *(Exod. 33:15–23)* **89**

Day 28 *(1 Sam. 1:10–12)* **93**

Day 29 *(1 Kings 17:20, 36–37)* **97**

Day 30 *(2 Kings 6:15–17)* **99**

Day 31 *(2 Chron 20:12, 15–17)* **103**

Day 32 *(Isa. 38:1–5)* **107**

Day 33 *(Ezra 8:21–23)* **111**

Day 34 *(Ezra 9:5–6)* **113**

Day 35 *(Psalm 51)* **117**

Day 36 *(1 Kings 3:6–9)* **121**

Day 37 *(Neh. 2:1–5)* **125**

Day 38 *(Hab. 3:17–19)* **127**

Day 39 *(2 Kings 19:14–19)* **131**

Day 40 *(Dan. 9:4–7, 9, 18–19)* **135**

Conclusion **137**

Foreword

Heather Torosyan's life proved the faithfulness of God. Her father and mother followed Jesus and taught their children to do the same. As a result, many people, including Heather and her family, sought the kingdom of God and His righteousness before all else. This led, as Jesus said it would, to an ever-widening circle of blessing.

I have been the happy recipient of that blessing. Years ago, when our children attended the same school and I knew her only slightly, Heather stepped forward to take me to ceramics class after I broke my ankle and needed a driver. When my ankle healed, we continued to drive there together, often stopping for a burger on the way back. Then Heather invited me to the Bible study she led in her home. We convinced her to go through Revelation with us. My souvenir from that study was when we got near the end and read about the hardships to come and God's triumph after all. Heather said, "So, you see, it isn't the end of the world. Well, it *is* the end of the world, but that isn't 'the end of the world.'"

Heather had a way with words, and she had a way with people. She was forthright, cheerful, and always pointing to her Savior. May you hear my friend Heather's voice in these, her private thoughts on prayers in the Scriptures. May they point you to the One who said to Heather and to each of us, "Come to me, all you who are weary and burdened, and I will give you rest. Take my yoke upon you and learn from me, for I am gentle and humble in heart, and you will find rest for your souls. For my yoke is easy and my burden is light" (Matt. 11:28–30, NIV).

ANNE MCKINLEY
Altadena, California
September 25, 2021

Preface

It has been my thought for a very long time that I need to be more diligent in my concentrated prayer—not the prayer of the moment ("Thank you, Lord, for letting that car miss me"), but the kind of prayer that is thoughtful and thorough. After getting a Moleskine notebook for Christmas from my daughter Sevan, I decided to use it for the purposes of prayer. I studied the prayers of the Bible, commented on them, and then prayed. My thoughts are here published as daily meditations. A space is left at the end of each day for you to write your own prayers. Let's start with Jesus's teaching about prayer and His prayers.

HEATHER JEAN TOROSYAN
February 21, 2010
Lord's Day

The Teaching & Prayers of Jesus

Day 1

But you, when you pray, go into your inner room, close your door and pray to your Father who is in secret, and your Father who sees what is done in secret will reward you. And when you are praying, do not use meaningless repetition as the Gentiles do, for they suppose that they will be heard for their many words. So do not be like them; for your Father knows what you need before you ask Him. (Matt. 6:6–8)

This teaching comes right before Jesus' example prayer, the Lord's Prayer. The main points are

- Prayer is between you and God.
- Don't make a show of prayer.
- Make a point to do it in private.
- You will be rewarded. (Jesus doesn't say how.)
- Don't use meaningless repetition.
- God won't listen more because you talk a lot.
- He already knows what you need.

The obvious question is, if God already knows what we need, why pray? I believe it is for our benefit: unburdening ourselves to One who has our best interests at heart, seeing the answers, and receiving some sort of reward—maybe peace of heart, maybe answers or miracles.

Lord, give me a praying heart. Help me to take the time and not just squeeze it in. Let me bring all my concerns to You. Let me see Your holiness.

MY PRAYER

_____

_____

_____

_____

_____

_____

_____

_____

_____

_____

_____

_____

_____

_____

_____

_____

_____

Day 2

Pray, then, in this way:
Our Father who is in heaven,
Hallowed be Your name.
Your kingdom come,
Your will be done,
On earth as it is in heaven.
Give us this day our daily bread.
And forgive us our debts, as we also have forgiven our
    debtors.
And do not lead us into temptation,
But deliver us from evil.
For Yours is the kingdom and the power and the
    glory forever.
Amen.
(Matt. 6:9–13)

In some ways, this prayer is difficult because we have
said it so much that we don't pay attention to what it
says. Even though I have known about this pitfall for a

long time and can teach on all the good things in the prayer, are my prayers fresh? Are they heartfelt?

What does the Lord's Prayer say? Jesus starts by saying, "Pray, then, *in this way.*" He had just finished telling His disciples not to pray like the Gentiles, with meaningless repetition. Yet the church repeats the Lord's Prayer, and, in many instances, it has been meaningless to the people who mumble the same words over and over Sunday after Sunday. Of course, the words themselves are not meaningless, but when words are repeated over and over, the mind can become disengaged.

If Jesus is not saying, "Pray this prayer," but, "Pray *in this way,*" what could He be telling us to do? Perhaps this:

- Praise: hallowed be Your name.
- Prayer for revival and obedience on earth.
- Request for our basic daily needs.
- Repentance: asking to be forgiven like we forgive.
- Sin prevention: help us not be tempted, and give us protection.
- End with more praise.

Under each category, we can be specific. It is good to read some psalms for the praise, as long as your mind is engaged.

When we pray that God's will be done on earth as in heaven, we are praying for people to be saved and for Christians to obey (and obey quickly).

Physical needs (our daily bread) are legitimate requests. We are not praying for the year, just for the day.

Then we should ask for forgiveness and tell God that we want to be forgiven the same as we forgive others.

After repentance, we ask for strength to obey, to avoid sin.

Then we praise again. "O Lord, our Lord, how majestic is Your name in all the earth" (Psalm 8:1).

Lord, I want to obey You as the angels in heaven obey You—quickly and without grumbling. Lord, help me keep away from things that tempt me. I know You won't lead me there, but I may wander off. Lord, Yours is all the power and glory forever and ever. Amen.

MY PRAYER

_____

_____

_____

_____

_____

_____

_____

_____

_____

_____

Day 3

My Father, if it is possible, let this cup pass from Me; yet not as I will, but as You will. (Matt. 26:29)

Jesus prayed this in the Garden of Gethsemane before He went to the cross. He prayed that if it was possible to avoid the cross (and still redeem mankind), that God would let it pass. The only way for us to be redeemed was for Christ to die. No other way was possible. He could have passed on the dying, but then we would still be lost in our sins. The prayer closes with Christ's acceptance, His dying to self before dying for us: *Not My will, but Yours.*

When we face a really difficult time, whether a physical trial or a test of our spiritual strength, it is OK to ask God to let the cup pass if possible. If the difficulty doesn't pass, God has chosen that method to gain His end. We may even assume that His end could not be reached any other way. We can accept it the same way Christ did: Not my will, but Thine be done. This is submission in the heart—dying to self, living for God. A struggle comes when we think the will being done is not God's but someone else's.

> I will give thanks to the Lord with all my heart;
> I will tell of all Your wonders.
> I will be glad and exult in You;
> I will sing praise to Your name, O Most High.
> (Psalm 9:1–2)

Lord, help me to die to self and live for You. Not my will! I would love it if my will were completely in sync with Yours. Let me not presume.

Lord, help me to obey You in all the little details. I ask you for opportunities to share Your good news with those around me who don't know You. There is so much You have lavished on us in terms of worldly goods. I thank You that all my life there has always been daily bread. Help us to share that wealth. Keep me feeding on Your daily bread. It is only fresh one day. Praise be to Your Name!

MY PRAYER

_____

_____

_____

_____

_____

Day 4

Father, forgive them; for they do not know what they are doing. (Luke 23:34)

Jesus said this after they hung Him on the cross between the two thieves. Notice how counterintuitive this prayer is. He was hanging on a cross and asking His Father to forgive those doing it.

Those who sent Christ to the cross knew that they were doing something wrong. How do we know? They didn't use the money that Judas returned to them because it was blood money. But did they know—could they have known—that they were crucifying the Lord of glory?

Jesus knew that they didn't know exactly what they were doing. He asked the Father's forgiveness for them. In fact, the blood He shed was for them, too.

One huge takeaway from this passage is that a forgiving heart doesn't have to wait for an apology or repentance. To say that forgiving people this way is impossible, that Jesus did it, but we can't, is sidestepping the issue. We see another example in Acts, where Stephen, while being stoned, asked the Lord to forgive the people killing him (Acts 7:60).

> "I love You, O Lord, my strength."
> The Lord is my rock and my fortress and my
>   deliverer,
> My God, my rock, in whom I take refuge;
> My shield and the horn of my salvation, my
>   stronghold.
> I call upon the Lord, who is worthy to be praised,
> And I am saved from my enemies.
> (Psalm 18:1–3)

Lord, give me a heart ready at all times to forgive, ready long before an apology is even (if at all) offered. Let me see that You are ready and waiting for us to repent, eager for our change of heart. Lord, let me have a heart like Yours.

MY PRAYER

_____

_____

_____

_____

_____

_____

Day 5

"Now My soul has become troubled; and what shall I say, 'Father, save Me from this hour'? But for this purpose I came to this hour. Father, glorify Your name." Then a voice came out of heaven: "I have both glorified it, and will glorify it again." (John 12:27–28)

This quote goes hand in hand with yesterday's passage. It was a prediction of Jesus' death. Although Jesus would later pray, "If You are willing, remove this cup from Me," He knew what was coming. Seeing what was in store for Him, He prayed, "Father, glorify Your name."

When we are going through hard times, we should have His mindset: "Father, in all things that I am going through, glorify Your name." Not my name, but God's name.

This prayer was a deliberate surrender of Jesus' own will and a recognition that all things should be to God's glory. "And we know that God causes all things to work together for good to those who love God, to those who are called according to *His* purpose" (Rom. 8:28). All things working together for good means they work for God's glory. As He healed the blind man in John 9, Jesus said that he was born that way "so that the works of God might be displayed in him" (v. 3).

In prayer, we should start with praise, giving glory to God's name. When we pray about our problems, we should also pray, "Glorify your name, O Lord."

> The heavens are telling of the glory of God;
> And their expanse is declaring the work of His hands.
> Day to day pours forth speech,
> And night to night reveals knowledge . . . .
> The law of the Lord is perfect, restoring the soul;
> The testimony of the Lord is sure, making wise the simple.
> The precepts of the Lord are right, rejoicing the heart;
> The commandment of the Lord is pure, enlightening the eyes.
> The fear of the Lord is clean, enduring forever;
> The judgments of the Lord are true; they are righteous altogether.
> They are more desirable than gold, yes, than much fine gold;
> Sweeter also than honey and the drippings of the honeycomb.

Moreover, by them Your servant is warned;
In keeping them there is great reward.
(Psalm 19:1–2, 7–11)

Lord, I ask that you would constantly remind me that in every situation I should ask for You to be glorified. Today I specifically pray, Lord, not my will, but Yours be done! Lord, glorify Your name in my life. Help me bring others to You. Your kingdom come.

MY PRAYER

_____

_____

_____

_____

_____

_____

_____

_____

_____

_____

_____

_____

_____

_____

_____

Day 6

Jesus spoke these things; and lifting up His eyes to heaven, He said, "Father, the hour has come; glorify Your Son, that the Son may glorify You, even as You gave Him authority over all flesh, that to all whom You have given Him, He may give eternal life. This is eternal life, that they may know You, the only true God, and Jesus Christ whom You have sent. I glorified You on the earth, having accomplished the work which You have given Me to do. Now, Father, glorify Me together with Yourself, with the glory which I had with You before the world was." (John 17:1–5)

The hour has come. For at least three years, Jesus has been saying the hour is not yet come. Now is the time. In yesterday's passage, Jesus prayed for the Father to glorify His name. Now Jesus asks that the Father would glorify Him so that the Son could glorify the Father.

Jesus had been given authority to give eternal life to those the Father had chosen. This authority was contingent on Jesus doing the necessary God-glorifying activity, i.e., dying on the cross. What is interesting here is how *eternal life* is defined: "That they may know [the Father], the only true God, and Jesus Christ whom You have sent." Eternal life is knowing God and Jesus whom He sent. Life is in Christ. Paul's desire was to know Christ and to know Him crucified (1 Cor. 2:2). That is life! That is abundant life. On top of this, material blessings are a couple of extra grains of sand on a two-ton load—not important, and adding no measurable weight.

In verse 4, we learn how we glorify God. Jesus glorified God by accomplishing the work which was given to Him. We can glorify God by doing the same.

The glory that Jesus asks God to give Him is the same glory He had with the Father before the world came into being. This makes me think that He is not speaking about the glory of the cross, but rather the *resurrection*.

> Who may ascend into the hill of the Lord?
> And who may stand in His holy place?
> He who has clean hands and a pure heart,
> Who has not lifted up his soul to falsehood
> And has not sworn deceitfully.
> He shall receive a blessing from the Lord
> And righteousness from the God of his salvation.
> (Psalm 24:3–5)

Lord, I want to know You more and more, to experience eternal life in knowing You. Lord, let me glorify You by accomplishing the work that You have given me. Clean hands and a pure heart come from confession. Lord, I need to not be so sensitive to others' behavior. Help me to shine your way despite other people.

MY PRAYER

Day 7

I have manifested Your name to the men whom You gave Me out of the world; they were Yours, and You gave them to Me, and they have kept Your word. Now they have come to know that everything You have given Me is from You; for the words which You gave Me I have given to them; and they received them and truly understood that I came forth from You, and they believed that You sent Me. I ask on their behalf; I do not ask on behalf of the world, but of those whom You have given Me; for they are Yours; and all things that are Mine are Yours, and Yours are Mine; and I have been glorified in them. I am no longer in the world; and yet they themselves are in the world, and I come to You. Holy Father, keep them in Your name, the name which You have given Me, that they may be one even as We are. While I was with them, I was keeping them in Your name which You have given Me; and I guarded them and not one of them perished but the son of perdition, so that the Scripture would be fulfilled. (John 17:6–12)

Several thoughts come to mind:

- Jesus manifested God the Father to His disciples. We should also manifest God the Father to those around us.
- The disciples had come to know that everything Jesus possessed originated with the Father. They truly believed that the Father sent the Son.
- Christ prayed that the Father would keep us in His name so that we could be one the same way the Trinity is One.

The last item is a huge prayer. We need to be willing to have this answered—that all Christians can be one with each other the same way the Trinity is One.

MY PRAYER

_____

_____

_____

_____

_____

_____

Day 8

Ascribe to the Lord, O sons of the mighty,
Ascribe to the Lord glory and strength.
Ascribe to the Lord the glory due to His name;
Worship the Lord in holy array.
The voice of the Lord is upon the waters;
The God of glory thunders,
The Lord is over many waters.
The voice of the Lord is powerful,
The voice of the Lord is majestic.
The voice of the Lord breaks the cedars;
Yes, the Lord breaks in pieces the cedars of Lebanon.
He makes Lebanon skip like a calf,
And Sirion like a young wild ox.
The voice of the Lord hews out flames of fire.
The voice of the Lord shakes the wilderness;
The Lord shakes the wilderness of Kadesh.
The voice of the Lord makes the deer to calve
And strips the forests bare;
And in His temple everything says, "Glory!"
(Psalm 29:1–9)

Here is what we have learned so far:

- Pray in private.
- Don't pray with meaningless repetition.
- Praise God.
- Pray for revival and obedience.
- Pray for daily needs.
- Pray with repentance for your sins.
- Glorify God's name in word and deed.
- Pray that our will and His will coincide.
- Forgive people while they are sinning against you, without waiting for them to repent.
- Jesus went to the cross to glorify God's name.
- Knowing God is eternal life.
- All Christians should be one.

MY PRAYER

_____

_____

_____

_____

_____

_____

_____

Day 9

But now I come to You; and these things I speak in the world so that they may have My joy made full in themselves. I have given them Your word; and the world has hated them, because they are not of the world, even as I am not of the world. I do not ask You to take them out of the world, but to keep them from the evil one. They are not of the world, even as I am not of the world. Sanctify them in the truth; Your word is truth. As You sent Me into the world, I also have sent them into the world. For their sakes I sanctify Myself, that they themselves also may be sanctified in truth. I do not ask on behalf of these alone, but for those also who believe in Me through their word; that they may all be one; even as You, Father, are in Me and I in You, that they also may be in Us, so that the world may believe that You sent Me. (John 17:13–21)

Jesus' first prayer for us in this passage is that we might have His joy made full in us. We can have this joy even though the world hates us. They hate us because we are not like them.

Jesus prays that we be kept from the evil one even though we are living in his territory. We are otherworldly, or at least not of this world, because we have become children of God.

Jesus prays that we would be sanctified in truth. Then He says that God's Word is truth. The road to being set apart (sanctified) is through the Word.

Jesus has sent us into the world in the same way He was sent.

He prays again that we would be sanctified in truth. There is no road to sanctification except through Him.

Again, Jesus prays not only for the disciples but for all those who will believe because of their word, that is, us. He prays that we would be one, that we would be in Him. The result of this unity will be the world knowing that God sent Jesus.

Jesus prays for our joy. Jesus prays for our sanctification. Jesus prays that we would be one.

Lord, I ask that Your joy be made full in me despite my circumstances. I know this is Your will because You prayed this for us. Lord, I want to be set apart for You, sanctified. I especially want to be one with You and therefore with other believers.

MY PRAYER

Day 10

The glory which You have given Me I have given to them, that they may be one, just as We are one; I in them and You in Me, that they may be perfected in unity, so that the world may know that You sent Me, and loved them, even as You have loved Me. Father, I desire that they also, whom You have given Me, be with Me where I am, so that they may see My glory which You have given Me, for You loved Me before the foundation of the world. O righteous Father, although the world has not known You, yet I have known You; and these have known that You sent Me; and I have made Your name known to them, and will make it known, so that the love with which You loved Me may be in them, and I in them. (John 17:22–26)

This is the end of our Lord's prayer for us. It centers on knowing God the Father and His Son, on us living in them and they in us.

In this portion, there are three *so thats*:

- Jesus prays that we would have unity with the Father, with the Son, and with each other *so that* the world would know that Jesus was sent by God.
- Jesus prays that we would be with Him *so that* we may see the glory which the Father gave Him.
- Jesus made known the Father's name *so that* the love the Father has for the Son will be in us, and Christ in us.

The Lord prays that we will be so much a part of Him that the world could look at us and know it. The relationship is there, and He wants us to be part of it.

> Sing for joy in the Lord, O you righteous ones;
> praise is becoming to the upright. (Psalm 33:1)

There are so many distractions and excuses that one feels justified in not complying. Lord, I know You give me no slack. Lord, I don't want to be annoyed. Let me see how sinfully ugly it is.

MY PRAYER

_____

_____

_____

_____

Day 11

Two men went up into the temple to pray, one a Pharisee and the other a tax collector. The Pharisee stood and was praying this to himself: "God, I thank You that I am not like other people: swindlers, unjust, adulterers, or even like this tax collector. I fast twice a week; I pay tithes of all that I get." But the tax collector, standing some distance away, was even unwilling to lift up his eyes to heaven, but was beating his breast, saying, "God, be merciful to me, the sinner!" I tell you, this man went to his house justified rather than the other; for everyone who exalts himself will be humbled, but he who humbles himself will be exalted. (Luke 18:10–14)

In the middle of a parable that Jesus was telling, He gave examples of two prayers, one right, and one wrong. The parable is about the Pharisee and the publican (tax collector). The religious one, the Pharisee, thanked God that he wasn't bad, didn't cheat, was just, was faithful to his wife, fasted twice a week, and paid tithes on everything. The publican/tax collector/ collaborator just bowed his head, beat his breast, and asked God, "Be merciful to me, the sinner!" It is this prayer—humbly admitting before God that we need His mercy—that God responds to by justifying the suppli- cant. "I tell you, this man went to his house justified."

Jesus says that if you exalt yourself, you will be hum- bled, but if you humble yourself, you will be exalted. So how does this affect our prayers? Certainly, there should be no listing of our accomplishments to God. We are to come before Him hat in hand, knowing that it is only by His grace that we aren't all simply consumed.

We know that we can pray for God's mercy on us because of what He did on the cross. We also know from the Lord's Prayer that we are to extend the same kind of mercy to others that we want to have extended to us.

> I will bless the Lord at all times;
> His praise shall continually be in my mouth.
> My soul will make its boast in the Lord;
> The humble will hear it and rejoice.
> O magnify the Lord with me,
> And let us exalt His name together.
> I sought the Lord, and He answered me,
> And delivered me from all my fears.
> (Psalm 34:1–4)

MY PRAYER

_____

_____

_____

_____

_____

_____

_____

_____

_____

_____

_____

_____

_____

_____

_____

_____

_____

_____

_____

_____

_____

_____

Day 12

At that very time He rejoiced greatly in the Holy Spirit, and said, "I praise You, O Father, Lord of heaven and earth, that You have hidden these things from the wise and intelligent and have revealed them to infants. Yes, Father, for this way was well-pleasing in Your sight." (Luke 10:21)

Jesus prayed this after the seventy disciples returned from their mission trip. They came back rejoicing. Jesus was rejoicing with them, but also in God's way of doing things.

What strikes me about this prayer is the spontaneous quality of it. Jesus bursts out with praise to God for His plan, for His way of doing things.

MY PRAYER

_____

_____

SECTION TWO

The Prayers
of Paul

Day 13

First, I thank my God through Jesus Christ for you all, because your faith is being proclaimed throughout the whole world. For God, whom I serve in my spirit in the preaching of the gospel of His Son, is my witness as to how unceasingly I make mention of you, always in my prayers making request, if perhaps now at last by the will of God I may succeed in coming to you. (Rom. 1:8–10)

Paul wanted to go meet the church in Rome but was not able to at this point. However, he prayed for them all the time. First, he thanked God for them. The news of their faith had spread throughout the Roman world, so, along with thanking God for the faith of people he had never met, he was also continually asking God that it be His will that he go to Rome. This can serve as our model for praying for churches around the world: thank God for them, and, if it is in our scope, ask God for an opening to visit them.

Paul's heart was big. He prayed not only for those believers who were his particular responsibility, but also for others whom God was using in the furtherance of the gospel.

Lord, today I pray for tribal churches in Ethiopia, that their witness would grow, that all of Ethiopia would know of them. I pray the same for the struggling church in the Ivory Coast, and for the completion of the translation of the Bible into the Bakwé language. Also, I pray for the church in Niger. These three African countries are where I have friends serving. I pray for the African Enterprise Foxfire youth teams, that they would effectively spread the gospel.

MY PRAYER

_____

_____

_____

_____

_____

_____

_____

_____

_____

_____

_____

_____

Day 14

I thank my God always concerning you for the grace of God which was given you in Christ Jesus, that in everything you were enriched in Him, in all speech and all knowledge, even as the testimony concerning Christ was confirmed in you, so that you are not lacking in any gift, awaiting eagerly the revelation of our Lord Jesus Christ, who will also confirm you to the end, blameless in the day of our Lord Jesus Christ. God is faithful, through whom you were called into fellowship with His Son, Jesus Christ our Lord. (1 Cor. 1:4–9)

Paul thanks God for the Corinthians always—

- for the grace of God given them;
- that in everything they were enriched, in all speech, and in all knowledge;
- that they lacked nothing;
- that Jesus would bring them blameless in the day of Jesus;

- that God is faithful; and
- that we are called into fellowship with Jesus our Lord.

Paul prays and is thankful to God for how He enriched the Corinthians in all speech and knowledge, because He is faithful.

Now let's put it to use by praying the same things for Christians we know.

MY PRAYER

_____

_____

_____

_____

_____

_____

_____

_____

_____

_____

_____

_____

_____

Day 15

[God] delivered us from so great a peril of death, and will deliver us, He on whom we have set our hope. And He will yet deliver us, you also joining in helping us through your prayers, so that thanks may be given by many persons on our behalf for the favor bestowed on us through the prayers of many. (2 Cor. 1:10–11)

This isn't a prayer of Paul, but he mentions the prayers of the Corinthians. He comments on how their prayers helped him and those working with him; it looks as though God's deliverance of Paul and his associates was helped along by prayers. Our prayers add to the mix—not that God couldn't do it without our prayers—He just does more or does less according to our prayers. Favor was bestowed on Paul and his companions according to the prayers of the saints. The result of answered prayer is more thanks to God.

There are many saints to pray for, so I will stop here and do that.

MY PRAYER

Day 16

For this reason, I, too, having heard of the faith in the Lord Jesus which exists among you and your love for all the saints, do not cease giving thanks for you, while making mention of you in my prayers; that the God of our Lord Jesus Christ, the Father of glory, may give to you a spirit of wisdom and of revelation in the knowledge of Him. I pray that the eyes of your heart may be enlightened, so that you will know what is the hope of His calling, what are the riches of the glory of His inheritance in the saints, and what is the surpassing greatness of His power toward us who believe. (Eph. 1:15–19)

Paul prays great things for the believers of Ephesus. He prays that God would give them a spirit of wisdom and revelation in the knowledge of Christ. He asks that their hearts' eyes would see

- the hope of His calling,
- the riches of the glory of His inheritance, and

- the surpassing greatness of His power toward us who believe.

What great things to pray for those we pray for: family, friends, Christian workers!

MY PRAYER

_____

_____

_____

_____

_____

_____

_____

_____

_____

_____

_____

_____

_____

_____

Day 17

And this I pray, that your love may abound still more and more in real knowledge and all discernment, so that you may approve the things that are excellent, in order to be sincere and blameless until the day of Christ; having been filled with the fruit of righteousness which comes through Jesus Christ, to the glory and praise of God. (Phil. 1:9–11)

Paul prays that the Philippians' love would keep growing and growing, but that it would grow in knowledge and discernment. He asks that this growth would keep going until the day of Christ.

This is so that they might approve the things that are excellent. It is so they could be sincere and blameless until the day of Christ—not *at* the day of Christ, but *until* the day. This is to result in their being filled with the fruit of righteousness that comes through Jesus Christ, and that results in glory and praise to God.

We can pray for our own love to grow and to grow this way, that we can approve what is excellent, so that we can be blameless. Let us also pray this for our loved ones.

MY PRAYER

_____

_____

_____

_____

_____

_____

_____

_____

_____

_____

_____

_____

_____

_____

_____

_____

_____

_____

_____

Day 18

For this reason also, since the day we heard of it, we have not ceased to pray for you and to ask that you may be filled with the knowledge of His will in all spiritual wisdom and understanding, so that you will walk in a manner worthy of the Lord, to please Him in all respects, bearing fruit in every good work and increasing in the knowledge of God; strengthened with all power, according to His glorious might, for the attaining of all steadfastness and patience; joyously giving thanks to the Father, who has qualified us to share in the inheritance of the saints in the light. (Col. 1:9–12)

Like Paul, we can pray for each other to be filled with the knowledge of God's will, which is what we would all like to know. But knowing His will is not enough. The next part of Paul's prayer here is the *way* we know God's will—"in all spiritual wisdom and understanding."

The purpose of knowing this is so that we will walk in a manner worthy of the Lord. That will result in-pleasing Him in all respects:

- bearing fruit in every good work;
- increasing in the knowledge of God;
- being strengthened with all power, not in small amounts, but according to His glorious might; and
- attaining to steadfastness and patience, joy-ously giving thanks.

MY PRAYER

_____

_____

_____

_____

_____

_____

_____

_____

_____

_____

_____

_____

_____

Day 19

Now may the God of peace Himself sanctify you entirely; and may your spirit and soul and body be preserved complete, without blame at the coming of our Lord Jesus Christ. Faithful is He who calls you, and He also will bring it to pass. Brethren, pray for us. (1 Thess. 5:23–25)

Here Paul prays for the Thessalonians' preservation in spirit, soul, and body. All three of these should be blameless at the coming of the Lord Jesus Christ. This is up to the God of peace. Paul prays that He would sanctify them completely. This is God's work, and He doesn't do half measures. He who calls us is faithful; He will bring it to pass.

Then Paul asks the Thessalonians to pray for him. Paul was not so high and mighty that he was above the need of their prayers.

We should pray for and trust God for complete sanctification (spirit, soul, and body), for ourselves and for others.

MY PRAYER

Day 20

We ought always to give thanks to God for you, brethren, as is only fitting, because your faith is greatly enlarged, and the love of each one of you toward one another grows ever greater . . . . To this end also we pray for you always, that our God will count you worthy of your calling and fulfill every desire for goodness and the work of faith with power, so that the name of our Lord Jesus will be glorified in you, and you in Him, according to the grace of our God and the Lord Jesus Christ. (2 Thess. 1:3, 11–12)

Paul begins by saying that he should always be giving thanks for the Thessalonians because their faith is "greatly enlarged." A little farther on in the same chapter, Paul says that he and his companions do pray for them. He asks that God would consider them worthy of their calling, that whatever desire they have for goodness and the work of faith, God would fulfill it so that Jesus would be glorified in them, and they would be glorified in Him. The end is always Jesus being glorified.

At the beginning of chapter 3, Paul asks that the Thessalonians pray for him and his companions so that the word of the Lord would spread rapidly, and that the word would be glorified. The gospel is the end.

MY PRAYER

_____

_____

_____

_____

_____

_____

_____

_____

_____

_____

_____

_____

_____

_____

_____

_____

_____

_____

Day 21

Now to the King eternal, immortal, invisible, the only God, be honor and glory forever and ever. Amen. (1 Tim. 1:17)

This is a burst of praise from Paul while writing to Timothy. Bursts of praise are totally acceptable!

MY PRAYER

_____

_____

_____

_____

_____

_____

_____

_____

_____

Day 22

First of all, then, I urge that entreaties and prayers, petitions and thanksgivings, be made on behalf of all men, for kings and all who are in authority, so that we may lead a tranquil and quiet life in all godliness and dignity. This is good and acceptable in the sight of God our Savior, who desires all men to be saved and to come to the knowledge of the truth. (1 Tim. 2:1–4)

Here Paul goes on to teach about whom we are to pray for and why. We should pray for everyone, with all types of prayers, requests, and thanksgiving. We are to pray for all who are in leadership and authority, from teachers and principals to presidents. The reason is twofold:

- So that we can live a peaceful life. (The leadership can easily remove tranquility from our lives.)
- Because it is good and acceptable in our Savior God's eyes.

A heart that can pray for despotic leaders is a heart that is acceptable to God.

MY PRAYER

_____

_____

_____

_____

_____

_____

_____

_____

_____

_____

_____

_____

_____

_____

_____

_____

_____

_____

Day 23

I thank God, whom I serve with a clear conscience the way my forefathers did, as I constantly remember you in my prayers night and day. (2 Tim. 1:3)

Paul is always thanking God for people. He says he thanks God *night and day*. He was constantly praying for others. It was where his heart was.

MY PRAYER

_____

_____

_____

_____

_____

_____

_____

_____

Day 24

Now the God of peace, who brought up from the dead the great Shepherd of the sheep through the blood of the eternal covenant, even Jesus our Lord, equip you in every good thing to do His will, working in us that which is pleasing in His sight, through Jesus Christ, to whom be the glory forever and ever. Amen. (Heb. 13:20–21)

In some of the New Testament's other letters, the prayers are for us to be filled with the knowledge of God's will, etc. Here we see that Jesus our Lord will equip us in every good thing to do His will, which will please Him. He commands, but He also equips. We should pray this way!

MY PRAYER

_____

_____

_____

The Prayers of the Old Testament

Day 25

Then Jacob was left alone, and a man wrestled with him until daybreak. When he saw that he had not prevailed against him, he touched the socket of his thigh; so the socket of Jacob's thigh was dislocated while he wrestled with him. Then he said, "Let me go, for the dawn is breaking." But he said, "I will not let you go unless you bless me." So he said to him, "What is your name?" And he said, "Jacob." He said, "Your name shall no longer be Jacob, but Israel; for you have striven with God and with men and have prevailed." Then Jacob asked him and said, "Please tell me your name." But he said, "Why is it that you ask my name?" And he blessed him there. So Jacob named the place Peniel, for he said, "I have seen God face to face, yet my life has been preserved." (Gen. 32:24–30)

The scenario here is Jacob is returning to the home of his family with all his possessions, his wives, and his children. Then he gets worried about how Esau is going to receive him, since the last time they saw each other, Jacob was cheating Esau out of his birthright.

Jacob spends the night before meeting Esau alone after having reminded the Lord that He had earlier promised, "I will surely prosper you and make your descendants as the sand of the sea, which is too great to be numbered" (v. 12).

The concept of wrestling with God and *prevailing* is just strange. If it had been an angel of God, sent to do God's business, that would make more sense. Whatever the case, Jacob struggled with God until God agreed to bless him.

This is similar to Jesus' story about the unjust judge who grants the woman's request for justice not because he was being righteous but to shut her up. Jesus said that God would bring justice quicker than the unjust judge for His elect who cry to Him day and night.

Jacob struggled all night but then asked God to bless him. I don't know if that was what the struggle was about all along or just the end of it. When we struggle in prayer, whatever our requests, we should not stop until all we want is God's blessing. We might be begging and praying for something else, but, in the end, we should be all about God's blessing, not what our particular prayer request was.

> As the deer pants for the water brooks,
> So my soul pants for You, O God.

My soul thirsts for God, for the living God;
When shall I come and appear before God?
(Psalm 41:1–12)

Lord, before all else I want to have Your blessing. I am very haphazard in what I pray for. I need the intensity of Jacob to not let go until I have that blessing.

Lord, You have blessed me with your salvation. Thank You! Thank You! Thank You! On top of that, I have my loving family: parents, husband, children, grandchildren, brothers, nieces, and nephews. And you have blessed us with physical wealth.

Lord, Your salvation is a certainly greater blessing than any of us deserve. It is from Your goodness, because of Your loving character. But You also have given us Your Holy Spirit.

If there is a lack, it is because I have let sin come in and make a home for itself. I need to want Your blessing more than the minute satisfaction that comes from getting my own way. My soul pants for You, O God!

MY PRAYER

_____

_____

_____

_____

_____

_____

Day 26

Then Moses said to the Lord, "See, You say to me, 'Bring up this people!' But You Yourself have not let me know whom You will send with me. Moreover, You have said, 'I have known you by name, and you have also found favor in My sight.' Now therefore, I pray You, if I have found favor in Your sight, let me know Your ways that I may know You, so that I may find favor in Your sight. Consider too, that this nation is Your people." And He said, "My presence shall go with you, and I will give you rest." Then he said to Him, "If Your presence does not go with us, do not lead us up from here." (Exod. 33:12–15)

In the previous chapter, Moses prayed that God would not wipe out the Israelites because He had promised (plus the Egyptians would talk). At the end of that exchange, it says that God changed His mind. This in itself appears to give fervent prayer much efficacy. I will leave it there.

Moses' last statement, "If Your presence doesn't go with us, do not lead us up from here," is a great prayer. Basically, Moses is telling the Lord that if He does not lead them, Moses does not want to go. He does not want the final responsibility of leading the people. God must lead them.

God had just promised Moses that He would lead them, that He would go with them and give them rest. God has also promised us that He will never leave or forsake us (Heb. 13:5). We can know this.

But consider Moses' statement that if God didn't go with them, he didn't want to go. Many times, we just plow ahead without paying attention to whether God is in our plans. We should submit ourselves so completely to Him that we don't want anything if it is not in His will.

Lord, help us to completely surrender our plans to You. We don't want anything if You are not in it or not leading us.

MY PRAYER

_____

_____

_____

_____

_____

_____

_____

Day 27

Then he said to Him, "If Your presence does not go with us, do not lead us up from here. For how then can it be known that I have found favor in Your sight, I and Your people? Is it not by Your going with us, so that we, I and Your people, may be distinguished from all the other people who are upon the face of the earth?" The Lord said to Moses, "I will also do this thing of which you have spoken; for you have found favor in My sight and I have known you by name." Then Moses said, "I pray You, show me Your glory!" And He said, "I Myself will make all My goodness pass before you, and will proclaim the name of the Lord before you; and I will be gracious to whom I will be gracious, and will show compassion on whom I will show compassion." But He said, "You cannot see My face, for no man can see Me and live!" Then the Lord said, "Behold, there is a place by Me, and you shall stand there on the rock; and it will come about, while My glory is passing by, that I will put you in the cleft of the rock and cover you with My hand until I have passed by. Then I will take My hand away and you shall see My back, but My face shall not be seen." (Exod. 33:15–23)

I love this section. First Moses says he doesn't want to go anywhere unless God leads him. Then he gets bold and asks to see the glory of God.

Do we want to see God's glory? God's response is to say that He will show Moses His goodness, and then He gives Moses just a glimpse of His back. The only amount of God's presence/glory Moses could handle was a glimpse of His goodness retreating.

God is so good that we can't even handle *seeing* it. But we should pray for it, desire it, and recognize that His glory is good, that His goodness *is* His glory.

Also, this is the section of Scripture where Fanny Crosby's 1890 hymn "He Hideth My Soul" is taken from.

> He hideth my soul in the cleft of the rock
> That shadows a dry, thirsty land;
> He hideth my life in the depths of His love,
> And covers me there with His hand,
> And covers me there with His hand.

MY PRAYER

_____

_____

_____

Day 28

[Hannah], greatly distressed, prayed to the Lord and wept bitterly. She made a vow and said, "O Lord of hosts, if You will indeed look on the affliction of Your maidservant and remember me, and not forget Your maidservant, but will give Your maidservant a son, then I will give him to the Lord all the days of his life, and a razor shall never come on his head." (1 Sam. 1:10–12)

When Eli accuses Hannah of being drunk after seeing her mouthing the words of this prayer, she answers, "No, my lord, I am a woman oppressed in spirit; I have drunk neither wine nor strong drink, but I have poured out my soul before the Lord . . . for I have spoken until now out of my great concern and provocation" (vv. 15–16).

Eli doesn't even ask what her request was. He only tells her, "Go in peace; and may the God of Israel grant your petition" (v. 17). Hannah went her way, ate, and was no longer sad (v. 18).

There are several things going on here. First, Hannah brought her troubles to the Lord—poured out her anguish, her concern. She was oppressed by her husband's other wife, who had several children and deliberately provoked Hannah over her barrenness (v. 6).

One cannot help but wonder about Hannah's deal-making with the Lord. People do this all the time, promising God all kinds of good behavior if He will answer their prayer. In this case, Hannah wanted a son so badly that she was willing to not raise him herself but to give him up to the temple to be a Nazarite.

Eli did not promise her that God would grant the request. He just blessed her with his own prayer, "May the God of Israel grant your petition." It was enough encouragement for Hannah, and she was no longer sad.

God does not despise the pouring out of our souls to Him. In fact, I believe He wants us to do that. "Cast all your care on Him, for He cares for you" (1 Pet. 5:7).

MY PRAYER

_____

_____

_____

_____

_____

_____

Day 29

"O Lord my God, have You also brought calamity to the widow with whom I am staying, by causing her son to die?" Then [Elijah] stretched himself upon the child three times, and called to the Lord and said, "O Lord my God, I pray You, let this child's life return to him." (1 Kings 17:20)

"O Lord, the God of Abraham, Isaac and Israel, today let it be known that You are God in Israel and that I am Your servant and I have done all these things at Your word. Answer me, O Lord, answer me, that this people may know that You, O Lord, are God, and that You have turned their heart back again." (1 Kings 17:36–37)

Here are two prayers made by Elijah. The first is when he is staying at the widow's house and her only son dies. She blames him, so Elijah takes the son's body, lays him on his own bed, then prays.

The second incident is when Elijah is praying on Mount Carmel. Elijah prays for God to answer his prayers so that the people will know that God is God and also know that Elijah is His servant.

When we pray for people, we should let them know *how* and *why* and *what* we are praying so that God gets the credit when He answers. We want to be identified completely with God, that we are His servants.

MY PRAYER

_____

_____

_____

_____

_____

_____

_____

_____

_____

_____

_____

_____

_____

_____

_____

_____

_____

Day 30

And his servant said to him, "Alas, my master! What shall we do?" So he answered, "Do not fear, for those who are with us are more than those who are with them." Then Elisha prayed and said, "O Lord, I pray, open his eyes that he may see." And the Lord opened the servant's eyes and he saw; and behold, the mountain was full of horses and chariots of fire all around Elisha. (2 Kings 6:15–17)

The army of the king of Aram (Syria) was feeling thwarted. Elisha always knew what he and his army were going to do, and all his military plans were failing. So the king of Aram sent an army to "talk" to Elisha. His servant saw the Syrian forces surrounding the city and was afraid.

When the army came down to him, Elisha prayed:

> As the enemy came down toward him, Elisha prayed to the Lord, "Strike this army with

blindness." So he struck them with blindness, as Elisha had asked. Elisha told them, "This is not the road and this is not the city. Follow me, and I will lead you to the man you are looking for." And he led them to Samaria. After they entered the city, Elisha said, "Lord, open the eyes of these men so they can see." Then the Lord opened their eyes and they looked, and there they were, inside Samaria . . . . He sent them away, and they returned to their master. So the bands from Aram stopped raiding Israel's territory. (vv. 18–20, 23 NIV)

This was a very effective prayer. Elisha prayed, and the whole Aramean army went blind. He prayed again, and they could see.

Before that, when his servant was stressed about the enemy army, Elisha prayed that he would be able to see the real situation—that the Lord's army was with Elisha. When we see troubles all around us, we need to pray for God's view of the situation.

MY PRAYER

_____

_____

_____

_____

Day 31

"For we are powerless before this great multitude who are coming against us; nor do we know what to do, but our eyes are on You." . . . . "'Do not fear or be dismayed because of this great multitude, for the battle is not yours but God's. Tomorrow go down against them. Behold, they will come up by the ascent of Ziz, and you will find them at the end of the valley in front of the wilderness of Jeruel. You need not fight in this battle; station yourselves, stand and see the salvation of the Lord on your behalf, O Judah and Jerusalem.' Do not fear or be dismayed; tomorrow go out to face them, for the Lord is with you." (2 Chron. 20:12, 15–17)

Here is the prayer of Jehoshaphat when Judah was being besieged by the "sons of Ammon, Moab, and Mount Seir" (v. 10). Jehoshaphat points out how God had given Israel the land as their inheritance, but now they were being attacked by an enemy that was too big to fight off, an enemy determined to take that inheritance away from them.

Very often we go to prayer when (and only when) we have no hope. "We are powerless before this great multitude who are coming against us . . . ."

God's answer to this prayer is spectacular. "Do not fear or be dismayed because of this great multitude."

There are many times when the Lord tells us to stand and watch. Look and learn! He will deliver. We need to recognize our weakness and leave it in God's hands. First, pray!

> O God, hasten to deliver me;
> O Lord, hasten to my help!
> (Psalm 70:1–2)

MY PRAYER

_____

_____

_____

_____

_____

_____

_____

_____

_____

_____

Day 32

In those days Hezekiah became mortally ill. And Isaiah the prophet, the son of Amoz, came to him and said to him, "Thus says the Lord, 'Set your house in order, for you shall die and not live.'" Then Hezekiah turned his face to the wall and prayed to the Lord, and said, "Remember now, O Lord, I beseech You, how I have walked before You in truth and with a whole heart, and have done what is good in Your sight." And Hezekiah wept bitterly. Then the word of the Lord came to Isaiah, saying, "Go and say to Hezekiah, 'Thus says the Lord, the God of your father David, "I have heard your prayer, I have seen your tears; behold, I will add fifteen years to your life."'" (Isa. 38:1–5)

This is an interesting prayer. Hezekiah gets sick, and Isaiah shows up to tell him he will die. But Hezekiah does not want to die.

This text is a great argument that the Lord listens to prayers, that He will change a set plan.

But Hezekiah is pouting, crying bitterly. Please, please, let me live! I have been good. God, let me live.

Some say that because his son Manasseh was born during this time, and he was the worst king ever, that Hezekiah was choosing the wrong way; it would have been better if he had died. Whether that is the case or not, I guess the lesson here is to be careful what you pray for. When the Israelites were complaining about the lack of meat, the Scripture says, "He granted their request but sent leanness to their souls" (Psalm 106:15). I shouldn't want anything *so much* that even though God grants my prayer, my relationship with Him suffers.

> Surely God is good to Israel,
> To those who are pure in heart!
> (Psalm 73:1)

MY PRAYER

_____

_____

_____

_____

_____

_____

_____

Day 33

Then I proclaimed a fast there at the river of Ahava, that we might humble ourselves before our God to seek from Him a safe journey for us, our little ones, and all our possessions. For I was ashamed to request from the king troops and horsemen to protect us from the enemy on the way, because we had said to the king, "The hand of our God is favorably disposed to all those who seek Him, but His power and His anger are against all those who forsake Him." So we fasted and sought our God concerning this matter, and He listened to our entreaty. (Ezra 8:21–23)

This is Ezra's prayer before he and his company leave on the journey to return to Israel. It is a prayer for protection on that journey. In fact, Ezra called a fast and time of prayer that they might humble themselves before God to seek from Him a safe journey for themselves, their little ones, and their possessions. They were carrying a great deal of treasure back to

Jerusalem, and without a military escort, they were a prime target for bandits on the road. Ezra had told the king that God was with them, so he didn't want to follow that up by asking for a guard to protect them against the many things that could happen. Verse 23 says that God listened to their entreaty. They did have to deal with ambushes, but the Lord delivered and protected them.

MY PRAYER

_____

_____

_____

_____

_____

_____

_____

_____

_____

_____

_____

_____

_____

_____

_____

_____

Day 34

But at the evening offering I arose from my humiliation, even with my garment and my robe torn, and I fell on my knees and stretched out my hands to the Lord my God; and I said, "O my God, I am ashamed and embarrassed to lift up my face to You, my God, for our iniquities have risen above our heads and our guilt has grown even to the heavens." (Ezra 9:5–6)

Once Ezra and company got to Jerusalem, the princes there confessed that the local residents and those already returned from exile (the people, priests, and Levites) had intermarried with all the evil people. This was not new for them; it was one of the reasons God had sent them into exile to begin with.

Ezra's response to the news was to tear his clothes and pull out his hair and beard. He had such high hopes—but what was God going to do with this continuing rebellion? Ezra repented for everyone, which resulted in everyone repenting. They put away the foreign wives and their children.

Despite their gross disobedience, God brought them back. However, God still wanted the sin dealt with. Everyone was brought to account.

What can we learn about prayer here? Repentance is the key. Ezra was ashamed before God, so ashamed that he didn't, he couldn't, lift his head. We should have such a sense of how grievous our sin is before a holy God.

> Be gracious to me, O God,
> according to Your lovingkindness;
> According to the greatness of Your compassion
> blot out my transgressions.
> Wash me thoroughly from my iniquity
> and cleanse me from my sin.
> (Psalm 51:1-2)

MY PRAYER

_____

_____

_____

_____

_____

_____

Day 35

Be gracious to me, O God,
According to Your lovingkindness;
According to the greatness of Your compassion
Blot out my transgressions.
Wash me thoroughly from my iniquity
And cleanse me from my sin.
For I know my transgressions,
And my sin is ever before me.
Against You, You only, I have sinned
And done what is evil in Your sight,
So that You are justified when You speak
And blameless when You judge.
Behold, I was brought forth in iniquity,
And in sin my mother conceived me.
Behold, You desire truth in the innermost being,
And in the hidden part You will make me know
    wisdom.
Purify me with hyssop, and I shall be clean;
Wash me, and I shall be whiter than snow.
Make me to hear joy and gladness,
Let the bones which You have broken rejoice.

Hide Your face from my sins
And blot out all my iniquities.
Create in me a clean heart, O God,
And renew a steadfast spirit within me.
Do not cast me away from Your presence
And do not take Your Holy Spirit from me.
Restore to me the joy of Your salvation
And sustain me with a willing spirit.
Then I will teach transgressors Your ways,
And sinners will be converted to You.
Deliver me from bloodguiltiness, O God,
The God of my salvation;
Then my tongue will joyfully sing of Your
    righteousness.
O Lord, open my lips,
That my mouth may declare Your praise.
For You do not delight in sacrifice, otherwise I would
    give it;
You are not pleased with burnt offering.
The sacrifices of God are a broken spirit;
A broken and a contrite heart,
O God, You will not despise.
By Your favor do good to Zion;
Build the walls of Jerusalem.
Then You will delight in righteous sacrifices,
In burnt offering and whole burnt offering;
Then young bulls will be offered on Your altar.
(Psalm 51)

David wrote this after committing adultery and murder, which means we know his guilt was real. We also see that his forgiveness is real: David's joy is restored. But he was contrite first. God makes the repentant sinner white as snow.

When we repent, this is how we should do it—a plea to God's lovingkindness. We must know our sin and acknowledge it, not explain it away or justify it. We must recognize that it is God whom we sin against, although people can be damaged along the way (e.g., Uriah the Hittite). We confess truthfully, with no back on it. No sugarcoating.

After this is done, we can "teach transgressors Your ways, and sinners will be converted to You" (v. 13). A life that has no sin left unconfessed is one that naturally loves to share the gospel—and it can be done with no hypocrisy.

MY PRAYER

_____

_____

_____

_____

_____

Day 36

Then Solomon said, "You have shown great loving-kindness to Your servant David my father, according as he walked before You in truth and righteousness and uprightness of heart toward You; and You have reserved for him this great lovingkindness, that You have given him a son to sit on his throne, as it is this day. Now, O Lord my God, You have made Your servant king in place of my father David, yet I am but a little child; I do not know how to go out or come in. Your servant is in the midst of Your people which You have chosen, a great people who are too many to be numbered or counted. So give Your servant an understanding heart to judge Your people to discern between good and evil. For who is able to judge this great people of Yours?" (1 Kings 3:6–9)

When Solomon became king, he was not immediately great. Here, just as his kingdom was being established, he offered ten burnt offerings at the high place in

Gibeon. This is followed by his famous Q&A with God in a dream. In this dream, God asked Solomon to pick what he wanted Him to give him. Solomon recognized his position as coming from God's hand, not his own merit. Solomon's response is like a prayer (vv. 6–9).

God answered this dream prayer in spades. He gave wisdom to Solomon like no other before or since. He also added riches and honor to him, without being asked, and promised that Solomon's life would be prolonged if he walked in God's way like his father David. It appears as though dreams can be considered prayers, perhaps because what is truly in the heart comes out in dreams.

James says that if anyone lacks wisdom, let him ask of God, "who gives to all generously without reproach, and it will be given to him" (James 1:5). The condition on this prayer for wisdom is that we need to ask in total faith, without a doubt. When we ask God for wisdom while doubting that He will give it to us, we should not expect anything.

God wants us to have wisdom. He wants us to *ask* for wisdom. He wants us to implicitly *believe* that He will give us wisdom. It all comes down to our trust in Him. As the old bumper sticker said, "God said it. I believe it. That settles it." This is one of the few things we can ask for and know we are asking in the will of God.

Solomon asked for wisdom to rule the Lord's people rightly. As a Christian mom, I, too, need that sort of wisdom. And He will supply it if I ask without doubting.

For as high as the heavens are above the earth,
So great is His lovingkindness toward those who
   fear Him.
(Psalm 103:11)

MY PRAYER

_____

_____

_____

_____

_____

_____

_____

_____

_____

_____

_____

_____

_____

_____

_____

_____

_____

I took up the wine and gave it to the king. Now I had not been sad in his presence. So the king said to me, "Why is your face sad though you are not sick? This is nothing but sadness of heart." Then I was very much afraid. I said to the king, "Let the king live forever. Why should my face not be sad when the city, the place of my fathers' tombs, lies desolate and its gates have been consumed by fire?" Then the king said to me, "What would you request?" So I prayed to the God of heaven. I said to the king . . . . (Neh. 2:1–5)

From the New Testament epistles, we know that we are to pray without ceasing (1 Thess. 5:17). This passage from the Old Testament is a great example of that in action. Nehemiah had no time to go meditate, fast, and pray at length. He was standing there before the king, who had asked him a question. He needed to answer *right away*—so he *prayed* to the God of heaven, then *said* to the king. God gave him the words, the right thing to ask of the king. The king granted his request.

MY PRAYER

_____

_____

_____

_____

_____

_____

_____

_____

_____

_____

_____

_____

_____

_____

_____

_____

_____

_____

_____

_____

Day 38

Though the fig tree should not blossom
And there be no fruit on the vines,
Though the yield of the olive should fail
And the fields produce no food,
Though the flock should be cut off from the fold
And there be no cattle in the stalls,
Yet I will exult in the Lord,
I will rejoice in the God of my salvation.
The Lord God is my strength,
And He has made my feet like hinds' feet,
And makes me walk on my high places.
(Hab. 3:17–19)

The times when we pray the most are when things are going wrong in our lives. Habakkuk's prayer was written during a time when things were physically very bad. This person is essentially without a reliable food source. He will have to forage to stay alive. Everything has failed—all the fruit, all the grain, all the meat sources. He is not joyful in these sad facts; he is joyful in God his Savior.

This prayer seems the opposite of the prayer of Jabez, where he asks the Lord to enlarge his portion. "Now Jabez called on the God of Israel, saying, 'Oh that You would bless me indeed and enlarge my border, and that Your hand might be with me, and that You would keep me from harm that it may not pain me!' And God granted him what he requested" (1 Chron. 4:10). But even in good times, we should have the mindset of Habbakuk, to hold everything in an open hand, so if the Lord sees fit to take away all our income, we can still exult in the Lord and *rejoice in the God of our salvation.*

> My soul waits in silence for God only;
> From Him is my salvation.
> He only is my rock and my salvation,
> My stronghold; I shall not be greatly shaken.
> (Psalm 62:1–2)

MY PRAYER

_____

_____

_____

_____

_____

Day 39

Then Hezekiah took the letter from the hand of the messengers and read it, and he went up to the house of the Lord and spread it out before the Lord. Hezekiah prayed before the Lord and said, "O Lord, the God of Israel, who are enthroned above the cherubim, You are the God, You alone, of all the kingdoms of the earth. You have made heaven and earth. Incline Your ear, O Lord, and hear; open Your eyes, O Lord, and see; and listen to the words of Sennacherib, which he has sent to reproach the living God. Truly, O Lord, the kings of Assyria have devastated the nations and their lands and have cast their gods into the fire, for they were not gods but the work of men's hands, wood and stone. So they have destroyed them. Now, O Lord our God, I pray, deliver us from his hand that all the kingdoms of the earth may know that You alone, O Lord, are God." (2 Kings 19:14–19)

Assyria has just conquered the nations around Judah and has come down to Jerusalem to do the same thing to them. The Assyrian armies surround Jerusalem. They call out in the Judean language so that all the people can hear that surrender is the better choice. Specifically, they say that no one else's god has been able to deliver them from the Assyrian army, and Judah's God won't be able to, either.

Hezekiah first went to the prophet of God and got a word from the Lord. He believed it and got ready for battle, only to be scared again by a letter from the Assyrian commander. This time, he took the letter himself to the temple and "showed God" what the blasphemy was.

God answered Hezekiah: "Because you have prayed to Me . . . I have heard you" (v. 20). That night God killed all the enemy forces. Sennacherib, king of Assyria, returned home, only to be murdered by his own sons while worshipping in the house of the pagan god Nisroch.

Going over the problem, surrendering it, and reminding yourself who we worship, like Hezekiah did when he prayed in the temple, is a huge help, whatever God's answer.

MY PRAYER

Day 40

Alas, *O Lord, the great and awesome God, who keeps His covenant and lovingkindness for those who love Him and keep His commandments,* we have sinned, committed iniquity, acted wickedly and rebelled, even turning aside from Your commandments and ordinances. Moreover, we have not listened to Your servants the prophets, who spoke in Your name . . . . Open shame belongs to us . . . . *To the Lord, our God belongs compassion and forgiveness* . . . . We are not presenting our supplications before You on account of any merits of our own but on account of Your great compassion. O Lord, hear! O Lord, forgive! O Lord, listen and take action! For Your own sake, O my God, do not delay, because Your city and Your people are called by Your name. (Dan. 9:4–7, 9, 18–19)

Here Daniel prays for the forgiveness of the people. It is a great sample prayer. We can always ask God to forgive us, but never because we are in any way worthy.

We ask Him to forgive us on the basis of His character alone. To have any worth at all, we need Him to give it to us. It is His attention that gives us our worth. It is only on the basis of His compassion that we have any hope whatsoever.

To God be the glory.

MY PRAYER

_____

_____

_____

_____

_____

_____

_____

_____

_____

_____

_____

_____

_____

_____

_____

_____

_____

_____

Conclusion

The prayer below is one I remember my mom teaching on so clearly. I did a calligraphy of it for her once. It is a prayer of simple thanksgiving for the fine Christians in Thessalonica, for their work of faith, their labor of love, and their steadfastness of hope in Christ. Believers like this are a joy to God's servants. We should remember to thank God for such believers.

> We give thanks to God always for all of you, making mention of you in our prayers; constantly bearing in mind your work of faith and labor of love and steadfastness of hope in our Lord Jesus Christ in the presence of our God and Father. (1 Thess. 1:2–3)